"The Constitutional Compass: Navigating National Principles"
How the Supreme Law Guides Society and Government

James Harris

All right reserved. No part of this publication may be reproduced, distributed, or transmitted in any form or by any means, including photocopying, recording, or other electronic or mechanical methods, without the prior written permission of the publisher, except in the case of brief quotations embodied in critical reviews and certain other non-commercial uses permitted by copyright law.

Copyright © James Harris, 2024

Table of contents

[Chapter 1](#)
[Chapter 2](#)
[Chapter 3](#)
[Chapter 4](#)
[Chapter 5](#)
[Chapter 6](#)

Chapter 1

The Birth of an Idea: The Historical Context

Origins of American Constitutionalism

The Constitution of the United States of America did not magically appear. Many different historical examples, intellectual concepts, and real-world examples all had a role in its development. To create a new system of governance, the founders relied heavily on Enlightenment ideas, British legal traditions, and their personal experiences as colonists.

Legislative Impact in Britain

An important influence on American constitutional theory came from British legal traditions, particularly the English Bill of Rights (1689) and the Magna Carta (1215). The Magna Carta laid the groundwork for the rule of law and due process by introducing the concept that the monarchy's authority was not absolute. By stipulating specific rights for Parliament and individuals—such as free elections, free expression within Parliament, and safeguards against harsh and unusual punishment—and by restricting the powers of the monarch, the English Bill of Rights carried these ideas even further.

The Philosophy of Enlightenment

The Constitution's authors were deeply impacted by the Enlightenment, a time of great intellectual growth in the 17th and 18th centuries. Thinkers like John Locke, Montesquieu, and Jean-Jacques Rousseau established the conceptual basis for contemporary democracy and republicanism.

Particularly influential were John Locke's views on natural rights, consensual governance, and the right to revolt against unfair power. Locke's statement that all persons had inherent rights to life, liberty, and property resonated powerfully with the American colonists, who strove to defend these rights against tyranny.

Montesquieu's notion of the separation of powers, expressed in his book "The Spirit of the Laws," called for splitting political authority among multiple parts to prevent any one party from amassing too much influence. This notion became a cornerstone of the American constitutional framework.

Colonial Experiences and Self-Governance

The American colonies' experiences with self-governance also profoundly informed the Constitution's drafting. Colonial charters and compacts, such as the Mayflower Compact (1620) and the Fundamental Orders of Connecticut (1639), created early forms of democratic administration and provided precedents for written constitutions. These texts underlined the need for governing by the consent of the governed and the requirement of written agreements to outline governmental functions and preserve individual rights.

Additionally, the colonial assembly and town meetings created a history of local self-governance and participatory democracy. The colonists were used to voting their representatives and controlling their local affairs, establishing a political culture that prized autonomy and civic involvement.

The Articles of Confederation: A Precursor to the Constitution

Following independence from Britain, the newly established United States functioned under the Articles of Confederation, enacted in 1781. The Articles marked the first effort to construct a national government, but they rapidly showed fundamental inadequacies that prevented efficient administration.

Weak Central Government

The Articles of Confederation formed a confederation of independent states with a weak central authority. Congress, the national legislative body, could not collect taxes, regulate interstate trade, or execute its laws. This failure to collect income and manage economic activity led to financial instability and trade conflicts among the states.

Lack of Executive and Judicial Branches

Under the Articles, there was no independent executive branch to implement laws or supervise the administration of government, nor was there a national court to handle conflicts between states. This lack of centralized enforcement and adjudication processes left the government inefficient in keeping order and handling disputes.

The Need for Reform

By the mid-1780s, it became obvious that the Articles of Confederation were insufficient for administering the burgeoning country. Economic turbulence, such as the post-war slump and Shays' Rebellion (1786-87), underlined the requirement for a stronger central government capable of preserving stability and defending property rights.

The Constitutional Convention of 1787

In reaction to the shortcomings of the Articles of Confederation, representatives from twelve of the thirteen states assembled in Philadelphia in May 1787. This assembly, originally meant to update the Articles, suddenly morphed into a full-scale endeavor to establish a new constitution.

Key Figures and Their Contributions

The Constitutional Convention brought together some of the most notable brains of the day. George Washington presided over the convention, providing his stature and direction to the proceedings. James Madison, sometimes nicknamed the "Father of the Constitution," played a major role in crafting the Constitution, giving important ideas and precise notes in the discussions. Alexander Hamilton, Benjamin Franklin, and Roger Sherman all made substantial contributions to the convention's work.

Debates and Compromises

The delegates confronted various controversial issues, including representation, the balance of power between the federal and state governments, and the regulation of trade and slavery. These talks led to some significant compromises:

The Great Compromise: Resolved the disagreement between big and small states by forming a bicameral legislature with proportional representation in the House of Representatives and equal representation in the Senate.

The Three-Fifths Compromise: Addressed the problem of slavery by resolving that three-fifths of the enslaved people would be considered for reasons of taxes and representation.

Commerce and Slave Trade Compromise: Allowed the federal government to regulate interstate and foreign commerce while barring any prohibitions on the slave trade until 1808.

Drafting the Document

Over many months, the delegates methodically prepared a new constitution. The resultant text created a federal structure with a separation of powers among the legislative, executive, and judicial branches, establishing a system of checks and balances to prevent any one branch from amassing too much dominance.

Ratification and the Birth of a New Nation

The draft Constitution was signed on September 17, 1787, although its approval was far from assured. It needed ratification by nine of the thirteen states to become effective. This created a violent discussion between Federalists, who supported the new Constitution, and Anti-Federalists, who believed it granted too much authority to the central government and lacked adequate safeguards for individual liberty.

The Federalist Papers

To urge the people and the states to adopt the Constitution, Alexander Hamilton, James Madison, and John Jay authored a series of writings known as The Federalist Papers. These articles defined the ideals underpinning the Constitution and addressed concerns about the possibility of political excess and tyranny.

Ratification and the Bill of Rights

The promise of introducing a Bill of Rights to defend individual liberty helped garner the necessary support for ratification. By June 1788, nine states had approved the Constitution, and it formally took effect. The first Congress under the new Constitution convened in 1789, and by 1791, the Bill of Rights was enacted, resolving many of the Anti-Federalists' concerns.

The development of the United States Constitution was a colossal accomplishment created out of historical necessity, intellectual ingenuity, and pragmatic compromise. Rooted in the ideas of liberty, justice, and democratic government, it developed a framework that has governed the country for almost two centuries. This chapter sets the framework for a closer analysis of the Constitution's structure, ideals, and lasting influence in the chapters that follow.

Chapter 2

Crafting the Framework: The Constitutional Debates

Federalists vs. Anti-Federalists: Ideological Clashes

The construction of the United States Constitution was characterized by intense ideological disagreements between two primary factions: the Federalists and the Anti-Federalists. These organizations had varied ideas on the nature of government, the allocation of power, and the preservation of individual rights.

Federalists

The Federalists, headed by personalities like as Alexander Hamilton, James Madison, and John Jay, campaigned for a strong central government. They thought that a powerful federal government was required to preserve order, provide for the common defense, and regulate business successfully. The Federalists felt that the Articles of Confederation had proved insufficient since the weak central government it created could not solve the urgent requirements of the new country.

Federalists envisioned the Constitution as a tool to combine the states under a cohesive and strong central authority. They highlighted the significance of checks and balances, a structure meant to prevent any one branch from obtaining too much power. The Federalist Papers, a collection of writings authored by Hamilton, Madison, and Jay, were crucial in establishing the Constitution and explaining the logic behind its provisions.

Anti-Federalists

In contrast, the Anti-Federalists, including famous personalities like Patrick Henry, George Mason, and Samuel Adams, were apprehensive of centralized power. They worried that a strong national government may become dictatorial and encroach upon the rights and freedoms of the people. Anti-Federalists favored a decentralized political framework that allowed great sovereignty to the states.

One of the principal complaints of the Anti-Federalists was the lack of a bill of rights in the original Constitution. They claimed that strong guarantees for individual liberty were important to preserve individuals from government overreach. The Anti-Federalist Papers, a collection of publications and speeches by different opponents of the Constitution, highlighted these concerns and asked for changes to restrict the authority of the federal government.

The Great Compromise: Balancing Representation

One of the most difficult topics at the Constitutional Convention was the subject of representation in the new national assembly. Delegates from bigger states preferred the Virginia Plan, which suggested a bicameral legislature with representation based on population. Conversely, delegates from smaller states backed the New Jersey Plan, which pushed for a unicameral legislature with equal representation for each state.

The Virginia Plan

Proposed by James Madison, the Virginia Plan proposed for a strong national government with three branches: legislative, executive, and judiciary. The idea envisioned a bicameral legislature, with the lower house chosen by the people and the upper house elected by the lower house. Representation in both chambers would be based on state population or wealth, favoring bigger states.

The New Jersey Plan

In response, William Paterson submitted the New Jersey Plan, which attempted to alter the Articles of Confederation rather than abolish them. This concept envisioned a unicameral legislature with equal representation for each state, regardless of size or population. It also includes measures to allow the federal government limited authority to tax and regulate trade.

The Great Compromise

The standoff between these rival plans was overcome by the Great Compromise, often known as the Connecticut Compromise, devised by Roger Sherman and Oliver Ellsworth. This settlement created a bicameral legislature with a House of Representatives based on population and a Senate with equal representation for each state. This system balanced the interests of both big and small states, allowing for proportional representation in the House and equal representation in the Senate.

Compromises on Slavery and Commerce

While the Great Compromise settled the question of representation, other controversial issues persisted, notably involving slavery and trade. These arguments resulted in numerous significant agreements that were needed to win the approval of all nations.

The Three-Fifths Compromise

A crucial topic of debate was how enslaved persons would be counted for purposes of taxes and representation. Southern states, where slavery was more common, wanted enslaved persons to be fully counted to boost their representation in the House of Representatives. Northern states, where slavery was less popular, resisted this proposal, stating that enslaved individuals were considered property and should not be included at all.

The Three-Fifths Compromise handled this problem by declaring that three-fifths of the enslaved people would be counted for both taxes and representation. While this compromise allowed for the approval of the Constitution, it also cemented the institution of slavery and underlined the fundamental disparities between North and South.

Commerce and Slave Trade Compromise

The Constitutional Convention also wrestled with concerns connected to the control of commerce and the slave trade. Northern states desired federal authority over interstate and international commerce, but Southern states worried that such control may harm their economic interests, notably the continuance of the transatlantic slave trade.

The Trade and Slave Trade Compromise authorized the federal government to oversee interstate and international trade but precluded any governmental restriction on the entry of enslaved persons until 1808. This settlement was a concession to Southern states, ensuring their economic interests were safeguarded in return for increased federal regulatory powers.

Drafting the Document

With these main concessions in place, the delegates proceeded to design the Constitution. The resultant constitution created a federal form of government defined by the division of powers and a system of checks and balances.

Separation of Powers

The Constitution defined the functions of the federal government across three branches: legislative, executive, and judiciary. Each branch was given unique rights and tasks to guarantee no one branch could control the government.

Legislative Branch: Composed of the House of Representatives and the Senate, the legislative branch was responsible for creating legislation. The House, with representation based on population, and the Senate, with equal representation for each state, created a balance between the interests of big and small states.

Executive Branch: Headed by the President, the executive branch was responsible for executing laws and handling foreign policy. The President's powers were tempered by checks from the legislative and judicial departments.

Judicial Branch: The judicial branch, chaired by the Supreme Court, was responsible for interpreting laws and ensuring they conformed to the Constitution. The judiciary's independence was safeguarded by lifetime appointments for judges, subject to confirmation by the Senate.

Checks and Balances

The Constitution established a system of checks and balances to prevent any one branch from obtaining overwhelming authority. Each branch had distinct rights to check the others, maintaining a balance of authority. For example, the President might veto legislation, but Congress could overcome a veto with a two-thirds majority. The court might declare legislation invalid, placing a check on both the legislative and executive governments.

The Constitutional Convention of 1787 was a key event in American history, characterized by fierce arguments and important concessions. The authors of the Constitution traversed complicated and controversial problems to construct a framework that balanced the necessity for a strong national government with the preservation of individual freedoms and states' rights.

The resultant constitution, with its sophisticated system of checks and balances and its devotion to the rule of law, formed a government capable of responding to new circumstances while safeguarding essential ideals. This chapter lays the foundation for a closer analysis of the Constitution's provisions, their interpretations, and their influence on the American government in the chapters that follow.

Chapter 3

The Blueprint Unveiled: Structure and Articles

The United States Constitution is a masterpiece of governance, aiming to construct an efficient and balanced government that could survive the test of time. This chapter goes into the detailed construction of the Constitution, analyzing its seven provisions and the revolutionary framework it developed to rule the new United States.

Article I: The Legislative Branch

Article I of the Constitution established the legislative body, known as Congress, which is split into two chambers: the House of Representatives and the Senate. This bicameral arrangement was a product of the Great Compromise, meeting the requirements of both great and small nations.

Section 1: The Legislature

Article I, Section 1 vests all legislative functions in a bicameral Congress, consisting of the Senate and the House of Representatives. This section stresses the necessity of a representative democracy, where laws are produced by elected individuals.

Section 2: The House of Representatives

Composition and Election: Members of the House are chosen every two years by the people of the several states. The number of delegates is depending on the population of each state, providing proportionate representation.

Qualifications: Representatives must be at least 25 years old, have been a U.S. citizen for seven years, and live in the state they represent.

Powers and Duties: The House possesses the unique right to originate revenue measures and impeach federal officials.

Section 3: The Senate

Composition and Election: Each state is represented by two senators, regardless of population, for six-year terms. Originally, senators were elected by state legislatures, but the 17th Amendment (1913) altered this to direct election by the people.

Qualifications: Senators must be at least 30 years old, have been U.S. citizens for nine years, and live in the state they represent.

Powers and Duties: The Senate has the unique ability to trial impeachments, confirm presidential nominations, and ratify treaties.

Section 4-6: Procedures and Powers

Elections and Meetings: Congress is obligated to convene at least once a year. The dates, locations, and method of elections are decided by the states, with Congress having the right to make adjustments.

Internal Governance: Each house regulates its proceedings, sanctions its members, and maintains a chronicle of its activity. Members are safe from arrest during sessions, save for situations of treason, crime, and disruption of the peace.

Section 7: Legislative Process

legislation and Resolutions: All legislation for producing revenue must originate in the House. A bill must pass both chambers of Congress and be signed by the President to become law. If the President vetoes a law, Congress may override the veto with a two-thirds majority in both chambers.

Section 8: Powers of Congress

Enumerated authorities: Congress is given certain authorities, including the authority to collect taxes, borrow money, regulate trade, coin money, create post offices, and maintain military forces. The Necessary and Proper Clause permits Congress to adopt legislation necessary to accomplish its stated authorities, enabling flexibility to meet future requirements.

Section 9: Limits on Congress

Restrictions: Certain powers are restricted to Congress, such as suspending habeas corpus unless in emergencies, making ex post facto legislation, and conferring titles of nobility.

Section 10: Limits on States

State Restrictions: States are barred from acting in international diplomacy, coining money, and imposing levies on imports or exports without congressional authorization.

Article II: The Executive Branch

Article II established the executive branch, led by the President, responsible for implementing federal laws and handling national affairs.

Section 1: The Presidency

Office and Election: The President and Vice President serve four-year terms. The Electoral College system is utilized for their election, with electors selected by the states.

Qualifications: The President must be a natural-born citizen, at least 35 years old, and a resident of the U.S. for at least 14 years.

Oath of Office: Upon entering office, the President must take an oath to faithfully perform the office and preserve, protect, and defend the Constitution.

Section 2: Powers of the President

Commander-in-Chief: The President acts as the commander-in-chief of the armed forces.

Treaties and Appointments: The President can create treaties (with Senate approval) and appoint federal officials, diplomats, and judges (with Senate confirmation).

Pardons: The President may give reprieves and pardons for federal violations, save in circumstances of impeachment.

Section 3: Duties of the President

status of the Union: The President must regularly tell Congress about the status of the union and suggest appropriate measures.

Law Enforcement: The President guarantees that federal laws are properly enforced.

Section 4: Impeachment

Removal from Office: The President, Vice President, and other federal offices may be impeached and removed from office for treason, bribery, or other grave crimes and misdemeanors.

Article III: The Judicial Branch

Article III established the judicial branch, including the Supreme Court and lesser federal courts, responsible for interpreting the law.

Section 1: Federal Courts

Supreme Court: The Constitution created the Supreme Court and empowered Congress to establish lesser courts. Judges keep their posts through good conduct, often meaning for life, to guarantee judicial independence.

Section 2: Judicial Powers

Jurisdiction: The federal courts have jurisdiction over issues concerning the

Constitution, federal statutes, treaties, conflicts between states, and other defined areas. The Supreme Court has original jurisdiction in disputes involving ambassadors and states, and appellate authority in other situations.

Trial by Jury: All criminal proceedings, excluding impeachment, must be by jury and conducted in the state where the offense was committed.

Section 3: Treason

Definition and Punishment: Treason is defined as levying war against the U.S. or helping its adversaries. Conviction requires the evidence of two witnesses or a confession in open court. Congress chooses the penalty, although it cannot result in corruption of blood or forfeiture beyond the traitor's life.

Articles IV-VII: Federalism and Constitutional Provisions

Article IV: Relations Among States

Full Faith and Credit: States must recognize the public actions, documents, and judicial procedures of other states.

Privileges and Immunities: Citizens of each state are entitled to the privileges and immunities of citizens of other states.

Extradition: States must extradite persons accused of severe crimes to the state where the crime was committed.

New States and Territories: Congress has the right to admit new states and control territories. States cannot be founded inside existing states without approval.

Republican Government: The federal government promises each state a republican form of government and security against invasion and domestic violence.

Article V: The Amendment Process

Proposal: Amendments may be suggested by a two-thirds vote in both chambers of Congress or by a national convention convened by two-thirds of state legislatures.

Ratification: Proposed amendments must be approved by three-fourths of state legislatures or conventions in three-fourths of the states.

Article VI: National Supremacy

Supremacy Clause: The Constitution, federal laws, and treaties are the ultimate law of the nation, overriding state laws.

Oaths of Office: Federal and state officials must swear an oath to uphold the Constitution. No religious test is necessary for taking office.

Article VII: Ratification

Ratification Process: The Constitution requires ratification by nine states to become effective. This article enabled the transition from the Articles of Confederation to the new government system.

The framework of the United States Constitution, methodically created by the founders, produces a balanced and effective government via its seven articles. Each article sets forth particular duties, responsibilities, and powers, providing a system of government that safeguards individual rights while fostering order and stability. This underlying structure has allowed the United States to adapt and prosper through changing times, emphasizing the lasting wisdom of the Constitution. In the following chapters, we will study how these values have been understood, contested, and defended throughout American history.

Chapter 4

The Bill of Rights: Safeguarding Liberties

Concerned that the emerging federal government would infringe upon personal freedoms, Anti-Federalists pushed for the adoption of the Bill of Rights, a collection of the first 10 amendments to the US Constitution. The independence and dignity of persons in a democratic society are ensured by outlining essential rights and safeguards in these amendments. Emphasizing its importance in American constitutional history, this chapter delves into the Bill of Rights origins, ratification, and important clauses.

Background and Approval

The Request for Changes

While the Constitution was being debated for ratification, Anti-Federalists claimed that it did not provide enough guarantees for personal freedoms. Without a well-defined set of rights, they were afraid the new national government would abuse its authority and bring about despotism. In light of these concerns, several states want a bill of rights to be included in the ratification process.

The Duties of James Madison

After the Constitution was approved, James Madison, who had first been skeptical about the need for a bill of rights, became a prominent supporter of the amendments. He realized that introducing clear guarantees for individual liberty would help ensure the new government's legitimacy and answer the concerns of its opponents. Madison offered a series of amendments to the First Congress in 1789, drawing from different state constitutions and suggesting changes from the state ratifying conventions.

Ratification Process

The proposed changes were considered and revised by Congress before being delivered to the states for ratification. On December 15, 1791, the requisite three-fourths of the states passed ten of the twelve proposed amendments, thereby enshrining the Bill of Rights into the Constitution.

The First Amendment: Freedoms of Speech, Religion, Press, Assembly, and Petition

Freedom of Speech

The First Amendment bans Congress from enacting laws that abridge the freedom of expression. This guarantee is vital to democratic administration, enabling citizens to express their thoughts, criticize the government, and participate in public conversation without fear of censorship or penalty.

Freedom of Religion

The First Amendment provides two essential concepts addressing religion: the Establishment Clause and the Free Exercise Clause. The Establishment Clause bars the government from creating an established religion or favoring one religion over another. The Free Exercise Clause ensures people the freedom to exercise their religion freely, without government intervention, as long as such actions do not offend public morality or jeopardize public safety.

Freedom of the Press

Freedom of the press assures that the government cannot control or limit the dissemination of news, views, and information. This protection is crucial for a free and informed society, enabling the media to act as a check on government authority and providing individuals with the knowledge they need to make educated choices.

Freedom of Assembly

The right to peaceful assembly permits people to congregate and jointly express, advocate, seek, and defend their beliefs. This protection fosters the creation of interest organizations, political parties, and public protests, maintaining a dynamic civil society.

Right to Petition

The right to petition the government for a redress of grievances permits citizens to officially seek changes or communicate their complaints to government authorities. This right guarantees that individuals may directly interact with their government and seek solutions for injustices.

Rights of the Accused: Amendments IV-VIII

Fourth Amendment: Protection Against Unreasonable Searches and Seizures

The Fourth Amendment protects people against arbitrary intrusions by the government into their private lives. It mandates that searches and seizures be reasonable and, in most situations, authorized by a warrant granted upon probable cause. This amendment defends privacy and property rights, offering a key check on government authority.

Fifth Amendment: Rights in Criminal Cases

The Fifth Amendment offers numerous key rights for those accused of crimes:

Grand Jury Indictment: Serious criminal accusations must be considered by a grand jury, ensuring that there is sufficient evidence to go to trial.

Double Jeopardy: Individuals cannot be prosecuted twice for the same crime, guarding against recurrent prosecutions.

Self-Incrimination: The amendment safeguards persons from being forced to testify against themselves, ensuring that admissions are voluntary.

Due Process: The government must follow fair processes and respect legal rights before depriving someone of life, liberty, or property.

Takings Clause: The government cannot take private property for public use without appropriate compensation, respecting property rights.

Sixth Amendment: Right to a Fair Trial

The Sixth Amendment protects various rights to ensure a fair trial for criminal defendants:

Speedy and Public Trial: Defendants have the right to a rapid and open trial.
Impartial Jury: Trials must be conducted before an impartial jury of the defendant's peers.
Notice of Charges: Defendants must be notified of the charges against them.
Confrontation of Witnesses: Defendants have the opportunity to cross-examine witnesses testifying against them.
Compulsory Process: Defendants may force witnesses to testify on their side.
Right to Counsel: Defendants have the right to legal counsel.

Seventh Amendment: Right to a Jury Trial in Civil Cases

The Seventh Amendment extends the right to a jury trial to federal civil actions involving claims over twenty dollars. This amendment maintains the common law heritage of jury trials and offers a check on judicial authority by enabling individuals to participate in the administration of justice.

Eighth Amendment: Protection Against Excessive Bail and Cruel and Unusual Punishment

The Eighth Amendment outlaws exorbitant bail, excessive fines, and cruel and unusual punishment. This amendment attempts to guarantee that punishment for crimes is proportionate and compassionate, safeguarding people from harsh treatment by the state.

Other Essential Rights: Amendments II, III, IX, and X

Second Amendment: Right to Bear Arms

The Second Amendment preserves the right of people to keep and bear weapons. This amendment has been the topic of much discussion and interpretation, balancing the rights of individuals to self-defense with the necessity for public safety and control.

Third Amendment: Quartering of Soldiers

The Third Amendment bans the government from compelling anyone to keep troops in their houses during peacetime without their agreement. This safeguard recalls colonial frustrations against British policies and highlights the significance of individual privacy and property rights.

Ninth Amendment: Rights Retained by the People

The Ninth Amendment states that the enumeration of some rights in the Constitution does not indicate that other unenumerated rights are denied to the people. This amendment assures that the mention of particular rights does not contradict wider concepts of individual liberty.

Tenth Amendment: States' Rights and Federalism

The Tenth Amendment reserves powers neither granted to the federal government nor forbidden to the states, to the states, or the people. This amendment highlights the notion of federalism, preserving a balance of power between the national and state governments.

The Bill of Rights is a cornerstone of American constitutional democracy, enshrining essential rights and safeguards that define the relationship between citizens and the government. These first 10 amendments indicate a fundamental dedication to individual rights, due process, and the ideas of justice and liberty. By guaranteeing freedoms of speech, religion, and assembly, assuring fair judicial proceedings, and stressing federalism, the Bill of Rights has played a vital role in defining American culture and legal tradition. In the chapters that follow, we will study how these amendments have been read and implemented via key Supreme Court decisions and their continuing influence on American law and life.

Chapter 5

Interpreting the Constitution: Landmark Supreme Court Decisions

The Constitution's lasting strength comes in its capacity to be read and applied to a broad variety of situations throughout time. The Supreme Court, as the highest judicial authority in the United States, plays a significant role in this interpretation process. This chapter discusses major Supreme Court judgments that have affected the understanding of the Constitution, demonstrating how judicial interpretations have altered American law and culture.

The Role of the Supreme Court

Judicial Review

One of the most significant authorities of the Supreme Court is judicial review, the ability to interpret the Constitution and reject laws and acts that disagree with it. This authority was established in the seminal case Marbury v. Madison (1803) when Chief Justice John Marshall ruled that it is "emphatically the province and duty of the judicial department to say what the law is." Judicial review guarantees that the Constitution remains the ultimate law of the nation and offers a mechanism for checking the powers of the legislative and executive branches.

Landmark Decisions on Federalism

McCulloch v. Maryland (1819)

In this decision, the Supreme Court examined the balance of power between state and federal governments. The state of Maryland had sought to tax the Second Bank of the United States, saying that the federal government did not have the constitutional right to organize a bank. Chief

Justice Marshall, writing for the Court, maintained the legality of the bank on the Necessary and Proper Clause (Article I, Section 8). The ruling upheld the primacy of federal laws over state laws, saying that states could not interfere with legitimate federal activity.

Gibbons v. Ogden (1824)

This case concerned a disagreement over interstate trade restrictions. The Supreme Court concluded that the federal government has the unique right to regulate interstate trade under the Trade Clause (Article I, Section 8). The ruling, delivered by Chief Justice Marshall, invalidated state laws that interfered with federal regulation of interstate commerce, significantly expanding federal regulatory power and reinforcing the doctrine of federal supremacy.

Expanding Civil Rights and Liberties

Brown v. Board of Education (1954)

A landmark case in the fight for civil rights, Brown v. Board of Education challenged the constitutionality of racial segregation in public schools. The Supreme Court, under Chief Justice Earl Warren, unanimously ruled that "separate but equal" facilities are inherently unequal, violating the Equal Protection Clause of the Fourteenth Amendment. This decision overturned the earlier Plessy v. Ferguson (1896) ruling and marked a pivotal step toward desegregation and the broader civil rights movement.

Roe v. Wade (1973)

In Roe v. Wade, the Supreme Court addressed the subject of abortion rights. The Court decided that a woman's freedom to choose to have an abortion was protected by the right to privacy indicated by the Due Process Clause of the Fourteenth Amendment. The decision established a framework for regulating abortion based on the trimester of pregnancy, significantly influencing reproductive rights and igniting ongoing legal and political debates.

Defining the Rights of the Accused

Miranda v. Arizona (1966)

This landmark case established crucial protections for individuals accused of crimes. The Supreme Court ruled that suspects must be informed of their rights to remain silent and to have an attorney present during interrogations. These protections, known as Miranda rights, are derived from the Fifth and Sixth Amendments and are designed to prevent self-incrimination and ensure fair legal representation.

Gideon v. Wainwright (1963)

Clarifying the right to counsel, the Supreme Court held that the Sixth Amendment guarantees the right to legal representation for defendants in criminal cases, even if they cannot afford an attorney. This decision extended the requirement for states to provide public defenders to indigent defendants, ensuring that the right to a fair trial is upheld across the nation.

Protecting Freedom of Expression

New York Times Co. v. United States (1971)

Also known as the "Pentagon Papers Case," this ruling upheld the First Amendment protection of freedom of the press. The Supreme Court found that the government could not prohibit the New York Times from publishing secret papers connected to the Vietnam War, since prior restraint would violate the First Amendment. This case underlined the necessity of a free press in keeping an educated public and holding the government responsible.

Tinker v. Des Moines Independent Community School District (1969)

In this decision, the Supreme Court expanded First Amendment rights to students in public schools. The Court decided that children do not "shed their constitutional rights to freedom of speech or expression at the schoolhouse gate." The judgment affirmed the freedom of students to wear black armbands in protest of the Vietnam War, as long as their acts did not impede instructional activity.

Addressing Equal Protection and Due Process

Loving v. Virginia (1967)

This important decision invalidated state laws forbidding interracial marriage. The Supreme Court concluded that such statutes violated the Equal Protection and Due Process Clauses of the Fourteenth Amendment. The ruling declared that marriage was a basic right and that racial discrimination in marriage laws was unconstitutional, thus expanding civil rights in the United States.

Obergefell v. Hodges (2015)

In a key victory for LGBTQ+ rights, the Supreme Court declared that the Fourteenth Amendment compels all states to allow same-sex marriages and recognize such marriages conducted in other jurisdictions. The ruling underlined the principles of equal protection and fair process, declaring that marriage is a basic right that cannot be denied based on sexual orientation.

The Supreme Court's interpretations of the Constitution have fundamentally altered American law and culture. Through major judgments, the Court has established the balance of power between federal and state governments, enlarged civil rights and liberties, defended the rights of the accused, supported freedom of speech, and provided equal protection and due process under the law. These opinions show the changing character of constitutional law and the continual endeavor to apply the ideas of the Constitution to modern circumstances. As the judicial branch continues to handle new issues, the Supreme Court's role in interpreting the Constitution remains important to the preservation of American democracy and the safeguarding of individual rights.

Chapter 6

Amendments Beyond the Bill of Rights: Evolving the Constitution

The United States Constitution, although sturdy and durable, was meant to be a living document, responsive to the changing needs and ideals of the country. Beyond the Bill of Rights, the Constitution has been modified seventeen times, demonstrating the dynamic character of American democracy. This chapter explores major amendments beyond the first 10, evaluating how they have impacted the political, social, and legal environment of the United States.

The Reconstruction Amendments: Rebuilding the Nation

Thirteenth Amendment (1865)

The Thirteenth Amendment passed in the wake of the Civil War, outlawed slavery and involuntary servitude, save as punishment for a crime. This amendment marks a significant transformation in American culture, formally eliminating the institution of slavery and opening the path for future civil rights gains. Its passage was a key step in confronting the nation's original sin and starting the lengthy process of reconciliation and regeneration.

Fourteenth Amendment (1868)

The Fourteenth Amendment is one of the most important amendments in American constitutional history. It established numerous fundamental principles:

Citizenship Clause: It guaranteed citizenship to anyone born or naturalized in the United States, including previously enslaved people, assuring that states could not reject citizenship based on race.

Due Process Clause: It banned states from depriving any individual of life, liberty, or property without due process of law, extending the protections of due process to state activities.

Equal Protection Clause: It obliged states to offer equal protection under the law to all people within their territories, setting the framework for future civil rights litigation and legislation.

The Fourteenth Amendment has been the foundation for several historic Supreme Court judgments that have increased civil rights and freedoms.

Fifteenth Amendment (1870)

The Fifteenth Amendment attempted to address racial discrimination in voting by barring the federal and state governments from denying a person the right to vote based on "race, color, or previous condition of servitude." Despite its approval, African Americans faced considerable impediments to voting via discriminatory practices including literacy tests, poll fees, and intimidation, leading to the necessity for future civil rights measures in the 20th century.

Expanding Democracy: Voting Rights Amendments

Seventeenth Amendment (1913)

The Seventeenth Amendment shifted the election of senators from being selected by state legislatures to direct election by the people. This adjustment was part of the Progressive Era reforms aimed at decreasing corruption and promoting democratic engagement, making the Senate more responsive to the voters.

Nineteenth Amendment (1920)

The Nineteenth Amendment allowed women the right to vote, a momentous triumph in the women's suffrage campaign. The amendment was the culmination of decades of work and struggle by suffragists and extended political participation by assuring that gender could not be used as a factor for voting.

Twenty-fourth Amendment (1964)

The Twenty-fourth Amendment repealed the poll tax in federal elections, eliminating a substantial barrier that disenfranchised many low-income and African American voters. This amendment was a vital step in the greater civil rights movement's attempts to ensure voting rights for all Americans.

Twenty-sixth Amendment (1971)

The Twenty-sixth Amendment decreased the voting age from 21 to 18, reflecting the notion that people old enough to be recruited into military duty should also have the right to vote. This development was motivated by the setting of the Vietnam War and the activity of young Americans wanting a role in their government.

Modernizing Governance: Structural and Procedural Amendments

Twelfth Amendment (1804)

The Twelfth Amendment amended the mechanism for choosing the President and Vice President. It required electors to cast separate votes for each post, solving concerns that occurred in the election of 1800, when a deadlock between Thomas Jefferson and Aaron Burr led to a constitutional crisis. This amendment simplified the election process and attempted to avoid future electoral deadlocks.

Twentieth Amendment (1933)

The Twentieth Amendment, commonly known as the "Lame Duck Amendment," reduced the interval between the election and the inauguration of the President and Congress. It changed the start of the presidential and congressional terms from March to January, minimizing the "lame duck" period and enabling newly elected politicians to perform their responsibilities more immediately.

Twenty-second Amendment (1951)

The Twenty-second Amendment restricted the President to two terms in office, or a maximum of 10 years if they took the president mid-term. This amendment was a reaction to Franklin D. Roosevelt's unusual four-term presidency and attempted to prohibit any one man from having disproportionate authority over a lengthy time.

Twenty-fifth Amendment (1967)

The Twenty-fifth Amendment defined the rules for presidential succession and infirmity. It created the procedure for the Vice President to take the president in the case of the President's death, resignation, or incapacitation and provided a method for filling a vacant vice presidency. This amendment guaranteed continuity and stability in the executive branch during times of crisis.

Addressing Modern Issues: Recent Amendments

Twenty-third Amendment (1961)

The Twenty-third Amendment allowed inhabitants of Washington, D.C., the ability to participate in presidential elections by awarding electoral votes to the district. Although it did not grant full representation in Congress, this amendment acknowledged the political rights of D.C. citizens in the voting process.

Twenty-seventh Amendment (1992)

Originally proposed in 1789, the Twenty-seventh Amendment forbids any measure that affects the salary for members of Congress from taking effect until after the next election. This amendment intends to eliminate conflicts of interest and guarantee that politicians cannot offer themselves rapid salary hikes.

Conclusion

The amendments beyond the Bill of Rights demonstrate the developing character of the United States Constitution and its flexibility to respond to the nation's changing beliefs and needs. From the Reconstruction Amendments that tried to reconstruct and redefine the country after the Civil War, to amendments increasing voting rights and modernizing government structures, each amendment has contributed to the continuing growth and refinement of American democracy. These modifications illustrate the flexibility and resilience of the Constitution, proving its potential to confront new problems and safeguard the values of justice, equality, and governance for future generations.

www.ingramcontent.com/pod-product-compliance
Lightning Source LLC
Chambersburg PA
CBHW050240230526
45470CB00005B/2047